Awesome Art

Clay Art

Jeanette Ryall

WINDMILL
BOOKS

New York

Published in 2013 by Windmill Books, An Imprint of Rosen Publishing
29 East 21st Street, New York, NY10010

Produced for Windmill Books by Calcium Creative Ltd
Editor for Calcium Creative Ltd: Sarah Eason
US Editor: Sara Antill
Designer and Modelmaker: Jeanette Ryall

Photo Credits: Cover: Jeanette Ryall r, Shutterstock Originalpunkt l. Inside: pp. 4–5: Tudor Photography;
pp. 6–7: (steps) Tudor Photography; p. 7: (main) Tudor Photography; pp. 8–9: (steps) Tudor Photography;
p. 9: (main) Tudor Photography; pp. 10–11: (steps) Tudor Photography; p. 11: (main) Tudor Photography;
pp. 12: (main) Tudor Photography; pp. 12–13: (steps) Tudor Photography; p. 13: (main) Tudor Photography;
pp. 14: (main) Tudor Photography; pp. 14–15: (steps) Jeanette Ryall; p. 15: (main) Tudor Photography;
p. 16: (main) Tudor Photography; pp. 16–17: (steps) Tudor Photography; pp. 18: (steps) Tudor Photography;
p. 19: (main) Tudor Photography; p. 21: (steps) Tudor Photography, (main) Tudor Photography; p. 22: (main)
Tudor Photography; pp. 22–23: (steps) Tudor Photography; p. 23: (main) Tudor Photography; pp. 24–25: (steps)
Tudor Photography; p. 25: (main) Tudor Photography; pp. 26–27: (steps) Tudor Photography; p. 27: (main) Tudor
Photography; pp. 28–29: (steps) Tudor Photography; p. 29: (main) Tudor Photography.

Library of Congress Cataloging-in-Publication Data

Ryall, Jeanette.
 Clay art / by Jeanette Ryall.
    p. cm — (Awesome art)
 Includes index.
 ISBN 978-1-4488-8085-0 (library binding) — ISBN 978-1-4488-8138-3 (pbk.) —
ISBN 978-1-4488-8144-4 (6-pack)
 1. Modeling—Juvenile literature. I. Title.
 TT916.R93 2013
 731.4'2—dc23

                                   2012003422

Manufactured in the United States of America

CPSIA Compliance Information: Batch #B3S12WM: For Further Information contact
Windmill Books, New York, New York at 1-866-478-0556

Contents

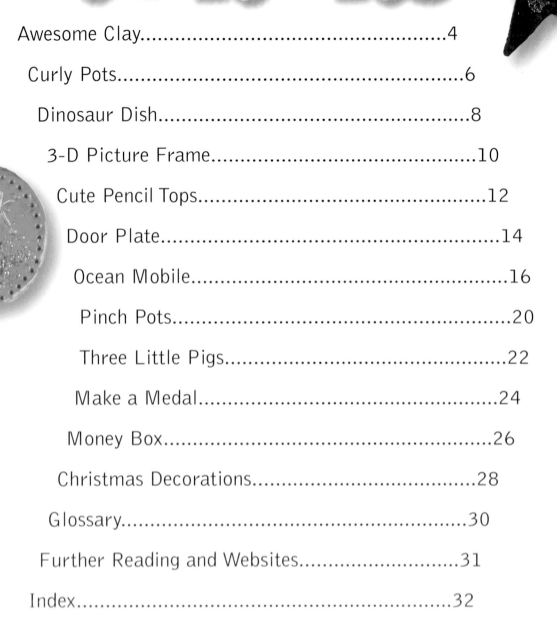

Awesome Clay

Clay can be shaped into the most incredible art! You can create fantastic pots, money boxes, door plates, medals, mobiles, and much, much more.

In this book we'll show you how amazing clay art can be.

NOTE Some clay hardens when left to dry in the air. We recommend that you use this kind of clay to make your clay projects. Some clay must be baked in a special, very hot oven, called a kiln, to harden. If you want to use this kind of clay, first check with an adult, such as an Art teacher. Be sure to use the correct kind of glaze for the type of clay you use.

You Will Need:

All the items you will need for each activity are listed on the following pages in a "You Will Need" box, like this one. Read these boxes carefully before you start to make sure that you have everything you need.

Before you start ...

• Ask your parent or caretaker for **permission** to use the equipment and space you will need for each activity.

• Find an apron to cover your clothes, or wear old clothes that you don't mind getting dirty.

• Ask an adult to help you with any of the activities that require cutting or cooking.

CURLY POTS

You Will Need:

- clay • bowl
- plastic wrap
- paintbrush
- clay **glaze**
- paints • water

Line a bowl with plastic wrap. From clay, roll out some long, thin sausage shapes, then coil them into **spirals**. Line the bowl with them.

Moisten your finger with a little water, then smooth the coils flat. Don't press too hard. Leave the clay to dry.

Make the **base** for your pot by rolling out one long sausage shape. Coil it into a small tower, as shown above. Leave it to dry.

4

Once the clay pot is dry, paint on a **design**. Use lots of different colors to make your pot bright. Paint the inside and base of the pot bright blue.

5

Leave the pot to dry, then stand the pot on the base. Paint your pot with glaze to give it a fantastic, shiny finish.

TOP TIP
You can create lots of different pots by changing the size or shape of the bowl that you use.

Dinosaur Dish

You Will Need:

- clay
- rolling pin
- water
- paints
- paintbrush
- modeling knife
- pencil
- glaze
- bowl
- plastic wrap

1

Roll out a large section of clay. It should be a little bigger than the bowl you are using in step 2.

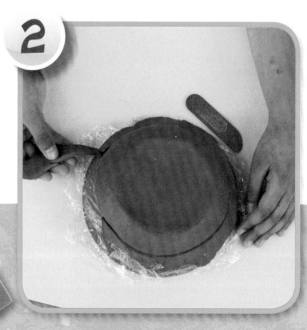

2

Cover your bowl with plastic wrap, then lay the rolled clay section over it. Use your modeling knife to cut off the **excess** around the edge. Leave the shape to harden.

3

Lift out the plastic wrap and remove your clay bowl shape. Shape a dinosaur head and tail from clay. Wet your finger with water, then use it to **seal** the head and tail to either side of the bowl.

4

Use a pencil to draw eyes and a mouth onto your dinosaur's head. Cut out some clay triangles. Attach them to the dinosaur's head and tail, and to the **rim** of the dish.

5

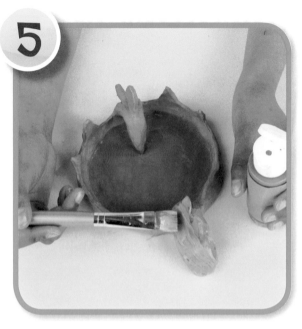

Leave your dinosaur dish to dry until it is hard. Then paint it with a dark green on the inside, and a light green on the outside. Use dark green for the triangles and add red or orange spots.

TOP TIP

Make your dinosaur shiny by painting it with glaze.

3-D Picture Frame

You Will Need:

- modeling knife • pencil
- metal ruler • paints
- paintbrush • clay
- glaze • glitter glue
- rolling pin

Roll out some clay around 6 inches (15 cm) wide. Use a ruler and a modeling knife to cut out a rectangle for your frame.

TOP TIP

You can use **metallic** paints to give your frame extra sparkle.

Use the ruler and the modeling knife to cut out a rectangle around 4 inches (10 cm) wide by 3 inches (8 cm) high from inside the picture frame.

3

Shape some stars, pebbles, an octopus, and other undersea shapes from clay. Attach them to your frame. Use a pencil to prick lots of tiny holes into the clay frame.

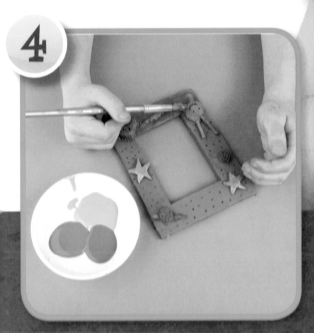

4

Once the frame is completely dry, you can paint it. Leave it to dry once more, then add glitter glue to your frame. Finally paint the picture frame with glaze.

TOP TIP
Put a favorite picture inside your clay frame.

Cute Pencil Tops

You Will Need:

- clay • modeling knife
- paints • paintbrush
- **garlic press** • water
- glaze • pencil

Top Tip
Finish your pencil top with a layer of glaze.

1

Cut a section of clay, then roll out one short sausage shape, one large ball, and two smaller balls. These will form the head of the pencil top.

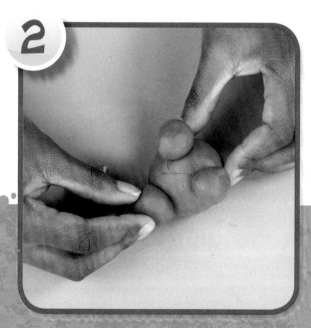

2

Press the two smaller balls to the top of the larger ball to form the eyes. Press on the sausage shape to form the nose. Put to one side.

3

Press a small ball of clay into your garlic press, then squeeze it shut to force the clay through the holes. This will create the hair for your pencil top head!

4

Wet your finger with a little water, then press the clay hair to the top of the pencil top head. Push a pencil into the base of the head to make a hole. Leave the head to dry.

5

Now you can paint your pencil top. Use bright colors, such as yellow for the skin, blue hair, and lots of red spots. Place the head onto the top of your pencil.

DOOR PLATE

You Will Need:

- clay • metal ruler
- modeling knife
- metallic paints and colorful paints
- paintbrush
- pencil

Roll out a large, thick section of clay. Cut out a rectangle around 4 inches (10 cm) wide by 3 inches (8 cm) high.

Use your modeling knife to cut a zigzag pattern into the top and bottom edges of the rectangle, as shown in the photograph above.

14

3

Use a pencil to draw a design around the edge of your rectangle. Use the pencil to write your name onto the door plate. Leave it to dry.

TOP TIP

Why not make another door frame with the word "enter" written on it?

4

Once dry, you can paint your door frame. Try a glittery gold paint for the edges and a bright blue for the center to make the door frame really stand out on your door.

OCean MOBiLe

You Will Need:

- clay • pencil • rolling pin
- modeling knife • round cookie cutter • star-shaped cookie cutter • paints
- paintbrush • two straws
- ribbon • scissors
- sticky tape

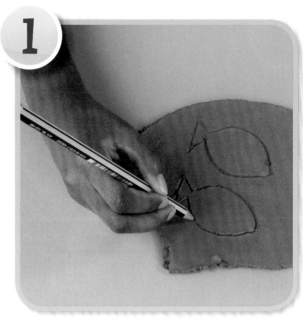

1

Roll out a section of clay, then use a pencil to draw two fish shapes into the clay. Cut out the fish shapes with your modeling knife.

2

Use the pencil to draw the scales, mouths, and fins onto the fish shapes. Make a hole for the eyes and another hole near the top of the fish. Leave to dry.

On another section of clay, draw two octopus shapes. Make a hole in each shape with your pencil. Cut out the shapes.

Roll out one more section of clay and use the round cookie cutter to cut one circle. Use a pencil to make a hole in the top of the circle.

Roll out another flat section of clay and draw some **coral** shapes onto it. Make a hole in each shape with the pencil. Cut out the shapes using your modeling knife.

Use the star-shaped cookie cutter to cut out a star. Place the star on top of the circle. Use your pencil to press lots of small dots into the star.

7

Put all of the clay shapes you have made to one side and leave them to dry completely.

9

Tape your two straws into a cross and seal into position at the center with sticky tape.

8

Once your clay shapes are dry, you can paint them. Use lots of different, bright colors. Leave the shapes to dry completely.

10

Cut some pieces of ribbon. Thread them through the holes in your clay shapes and tie a knot in the ribbon. Tie your shapes onto the cross to make the mobile.

Thread a piece of ribbon through the hole of the clay circle with the star shape. Tie the ribbon to the cross.

TOP TIP

Ask an adult to hang your mobile from the ceiling.

PinCH PotS

1

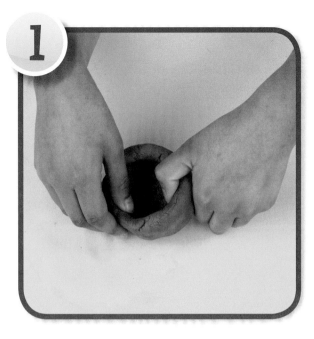

Roll a large section of clay into a ball. Press your thumb into the center and gently shape the ball into a pot using both hands.

2

Wet your fingers with water, then pinch the edges of the pot as shown to create a smooth, flat rim. Leave the pot to dry.

3

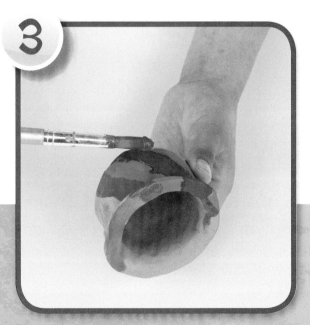

When the pot is completely dry, paint it with lots of bright colors. You could try a striped pattern. Leave to dry, then apply glaze.

TOP TIP
Use this **technique** to create cups and other small pots.

21

THREE Little PIGS

You Will Need:

- modeling knife
- paintbrush • glaze
- pink paint • water
- clay • pencil

1

From your clay, make one large ball and one long sausage shape. Use the modeling knife to cut the sausage shape into five sections.

2

Use the modeling knife to **score** the underside of the ball and the sausage sections. Wet the sections, then attach four of them to the underside of the ball. Attach the fifth to the front of the ball.

3

Stand the ball upright on the four legs. Use a pencil to make holes for the eyes and nostrils. Shape a curly tail and two ears from clay. Wet them slightly and attach to the pig.

4

Use these techniques to make a whole family of pigs!

Leave the pig to dry completely. Then, cover it with pink paint. Leave it to dry once more before applying lots of glaze to give the pig a really shiny finish.

Make a MEDAL

You Will Need:

- clay • rolling pin
- modeling knife • pencil
- star-shaped cookie cutter
- paintbrush • gold paint
- large drinking glass
- small drinking glass
- piece of ribbon
- water

Roll out a section of clay using your rolling pin. Press the large drinking glass into the clay to cut a circle. Twist the glass and press firmly to make sure you cut the circle cleanly.

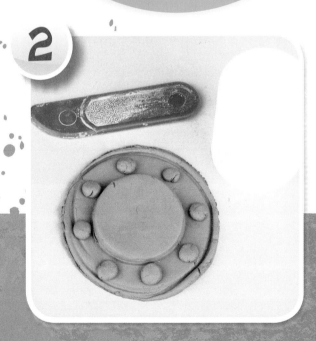

Use the small drinking glass to cut another clay circle. Press the smaller circle onto the larger one. Roll lots of small balls from clay, then arrange them around the edge.

Use your pencil to draw a small line between each of the small clay balls. Then carefully draw a line around the edge of the larger circle. Make a hole in the edge with your pencil.

TOP TIP

Tie the ribbon around your neck and show off your fantastic medal!

4

Roll out another section of clay, and use the star-shaped cookie cutter to cut a star. Wet the star, then press it onto the circle. Write "1st" on the star shape.

5

Cover your medal with lots of gold paint. You may need to apply a few layers. Leave to dry, then thread the ribbon through the hole in the edge of the medal.

Money Box

You Will Need:

- clay • rolling pin
- paints • paintbrush
- modeling knife
- water • glaze
- metal ruler

1

Roll out a flat piece of clay. Cut four rectangles measuring 4 inches (10 cm) by 3 inches (8 cm). Cut a slit in one. Cut two squares that are 3 inches square (8 cm²).

2

From the remaining clay, cut some small circles and triangles using your modeling knife. Roll up some thin coils of clay. Arrange on your flat clay sections as shown above.

3

Put the rectangle with the slit to one side. Use the modeling knife to score the edges of the remaining clay sections. Wet with some water, then position them to make a box.

4

TOP TiP

Let the clay dry slightly before trying to assemble your box. This will help stop the sides from collapsing.

Roll some long, thin sausage sections of clay, then use them to line the corners of the box, as shown above. Wet the sausage sections, then press them into the corners of the box to fix the sides securely.

5

Leave the box to dry, then decorate it with your paints. Don't forget to paint the rectangle with the slit. This will be the top of your money box. When dry, place the top on the box. Cover your money box with glaze.

TOP TiP

Keep your coins inside your fabulous money box.

CHRISTMAS DECORATIONS

You Will Need:

- clay • rolling pin
- modeling knife • ribbon
- star-shaped cookie cutter
- round cookie cutter
- pencil • metallic paints
- paintbrush • glue
- gold glitter • scissors

Use your rolling pin to roll out a large, flat section of clay. Make sure the section is not too thin. It should be around 0.5 inch (1 cm) thick to make sure the decorations do not fall apart when they are dry.

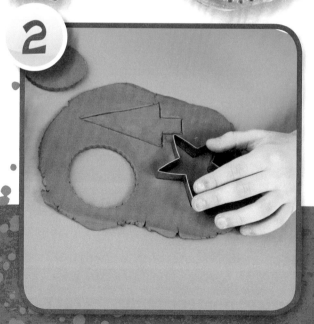

Use the star-shaped cookie cutter to cut out a star. Cut out a circle with the round cookie cutter. Use your modeling knife to cut out a Christmas tree shape.

3

TOP TIP
Use a **variety** of glitter colors for a colorful look.

Use the pencil to press a large hole into the top of each shape. Then press lots of smaller holes into the shapes to decorate them. Leave to dry.

4

Paint your shapes different colors, then leave them to dry once more. Cover the shapes with glue and gold glitter. Cut pieces of ribbon to hang your decorations!

GLossaRy

base (BAYS) The bottom of something.

coral (KOR-ul) Structures that grow on reefs under the sea.

design (dih-ZYN) A pattern or different shapes that make an image.

excess (EK-ses) Extra and not needed.

garlic press (GAR-lik PRES) A tool used to crush garlic.

glaze (GLAYZ) A liquid that gives clay a shiny look.

metallic (muh-TA-lik) Contains metals or looks shiny.

moisten (MOY-sen) To wet something.

permission (per-MIH-shun) To be allowed to do something.

rim (RIHM) The edge of a container.

score (SKOR) To cut small lines into something.

seal (SEEL) To fix something firmly.

spirals (SPY—rulz) Long, coiled shapes.

technique (tek-NEEK) Ways of doing something.

variety (vuh-RY-ih-tee) Lots of different types of something.

FuRtHeR ReaDiNG

Cuxart, Bernadette. *Modeling Clay Animals*. Hauppauge, NY: Barron's Educational Series, 2011.

Henry, Sally. *Clay Modeling*. Make Your Own Art. New York: PowerKids Press, 2009.

Kenney, Karen Latchana. *Super Simple Clay Projects: Fun and East-to-Make Crafts for Kids*. Minneapolis, MN: ABDO Publishing, 2010.

WeBSites

For web resources related to the subject of this book, go to: **www.windmillbooks.com/weblinks** and select this book's title.

INDEX